THE SHORT AND
BLOODY
HISTORY
OF
SPIES

Also by John Farman

John Farman

THE SHORT AND BLOODY HISTORY OF SPIES

RED FOX

A Red Fox Book

Published by Random House Children's Books
20 Vauxhall Bridge Road, London SW1V 2SA

A division of The Random House Group Ltd
London Melbourne Sydney Auckland
Johannesburg and agencies throughout the world

Copyright © John Farman 2000

1 3 5 7 9 10 8 6 4 2

First published in Great Britain by
Red Fox Children's Books 2000

Printed and bound in Great Britain by
Cox and Wyman

Papers used by Random House Group Ltd are natural,
recyclable products made from wood grown in sustainable forests.
The manufacturing processes conform to the
environmental regulations of the country of origins.

The Random House Group Limited Reg. No. 954009

www.randomhouse.co.uk

ISBN 0 09 940715 9

CONTENTS

PSST! WANNA KNOW ALL ABOUT SPIES?

Most people think of spies as dark, shadowy men with big brimmed hats, dodgy moustaches and no friends (or is that writers★?). Most of the time they aren't (and weren't) anything like that. For a start, there have always been almost as many women as men in the spying game, and for a second, nine times out of ten you wouldn't have known one if you met one. Just like zebras have a habit of wearing stripes so's not to stand out in the environment where they live, and chameleons change colour for just about the same reason, spies are most notable for not being notable. Let's face it, your teacher, your dentist, that funny bloke who works in the library, or even your own mum or dad could be one – and you would never know anything about it. Spooky or what?

★ *Male writers: Ed*

So What and Who is a Spy?

Spies are those guys who are paid to move quietly amongst one group of people to find out secret stuff that another group (the ones who pay them) want to hear about: spies are sort of professional tell-tales. So why would anyone want to pass on the secrets of those who appear to be their friends to people who appear not to be? Surely that's a really mean thing to do. Oddly enough, a spy can usually get away with anything: lying, cheating, stealing – even murdering, and still not be thought that badly of – it's all part of the game called espionage.

Most of the time spies spy for political reasons – because they don't like how another country runs its business. This was very much the case during what was called the 'Cold War' between the Soviet communist lot and the Anglo-American capitalists which started in 1945 as soon as we beat the Germans in the Second World War. To be fair, these spies were almost the most forgivable ones, for at least they believed that what they were doing was for the good of mankind. Whether they were right or wrong is not for me to say but, either way, practically every country in the world spies on every other country in the world – it's a fact.

Example

Despite the Soviet Union's rather unexpected fall apart in 1991, resulting in the dismantling of the infamous KGB, Russia now boasts four intelligence services and keeps squillions of spies in embassies throughout the world. Other sorts of spies, of course, don't do it for nice, moral reasons and they never did give a damn about high-flown ideologies like communism or capitalism. They're the ones who work purely for the dosh. This sort of behaviour is becoming more and more the case in big business, where huge amounts change hands for details about a rival's strategies or products. The recipe for Coca-Cola, for instance, has always remained famous as one of the most guarded and sought-after secrets ever, and rivals would pay a king's ransom for the hidden ingredient.

But . . .

. . . that's just the simple side of things. Have you ever heard of counter-espionage or of such a thing as a double agent? This is where it all gets a bit tricky. Counterspies or double agents are the ones that one side thinks are working for them, but really turn out to be working for the people that they are supposed to be spying on – or sometimes even both . . . a classic double bluff. They often give their clients (the ones buying the secrets) a whole bunch of false twaddle, simply to lead them away from the real plot. The best thing about this scenario is that the spy in question usually gets paid by both sides, a sort of double whammy. The worst

thing about this scenario is that when the people who first employed them or even the second people who employed them find out they've been double-crossed, they tend to be rather annoyed. That's generally how more than a few spies end up wearing stylish concrete boots, and being shoved over tall bridges into deep water and seldom heard of again (apart from the odd rather smelly bubble).

Mole Hunt!

Very often a person will stay in the same job for years while leaking little titbits of information every now and again to the enemy or business rivals. Not from the likes of hairdressers or garden centres, I must add, but companies where either the inside information is useful to another country (weapons etc.) or to a business competitor (car manufacturers etc.). These people are called 'moles', presumably because they operate 'underground' and presumably for the most part invisibly.

Good Kit

As technology develops, so do the tools that a country or company can use to spy on another. Real life constantly leaves James Bond with his 007 pants down. There are weeny little cameras that work in the dark, pin size microphones that operate all on their very own (without wires) and computers that can hack into others even though there seems to be no connection. These are all now commonplace. So much so, that really important meetings, political or otherwise, increasingly have to be held in sterile, unget-at-able plastic bubbles.

Old News

But trying to find out other people's secrets is nothing new, and nosy individuals have been trying to get away with such naughtiness almost since the beginning of time. This little book will attempt to trace espionage from its very beginnings, tell you who were the best and worst people at it, and give you a little bit of the day-to-day life of a fully paid-up spy.

EARLY DAYS

Spying has always been known as the second oldest profession. The first is nothing you need to know about.

The problem with spying is that it tends to be done in secret, so a lot of the really successful spying operations went on without anyone managing to write much about them – good for the spies but bad for history. Obviously, this becomes a bit of a problem when writing a book about the subject but there do seem to be a few names that crop up every time I dive into the deep and dusty records. Names like:

Sun Tzu (599 BC)

Just like everything else, spying seems to have begun in China. Try as I might, I can't find any records of espionage that go back beyond 510 BC, when a Chinese chappie called Sun Tzu, wrote a book called *Ping Fa* or, if your Chinese isn't up to scratch, *The Principles of War*.

It was all about how to get yourself a proper secret service with spies and stuff and how to use them when

having a war – which seemed to be about all the time in ancient China. It was so good, this book, that it became compulsory reading for Chinese generals and military men until the time of Pearl Harbor in December 1941 when American scholars realised that the tactics of the devastating attack by the Japanese on their fleet came straight from the pages of Ping Fa and thought that it might be quite a smart idea to get it translated into American (or even English) as well. One of the most famous lines in the book went something like: 'Those who know the enemy as well as themselves, will never suffer defeat'. Also: 'Foreknowledge enables sovereigns and commanders to strike and conquer and achieve things beyond the reach of ordinary men'.

Pay attention to this bit because I'm going test you on it later.

Sun Tzu came from Ch'i but lived in Wu. King Ho Lu read Ping Fa and made Sun Tzu head of his troops. Sun Tzu defeated Ch'u and entered the capital Ying before turning his attention to Ch'i and Ching. Clear? Good.

Sun Tzu described every type of spy and claimed that they must be honoured above everybody else in the land. He liked the idea of seeking out enemy spies and being so nice to them (free takeaways etc.) that they'd come over to his side and spy on their old bosses while telling them porkies (sweet and sour) about his lot.

Test
Without looking:
Who was Ho Lu?
Who read Ping Fa?
What was the capital of Ch'u?
Who came from Wu?
And, most of all ... Wu cares?

Alexander the Great (356 BC)

The next person I turned up was Alexander the Great, of all people. Alexander was the son of the mighty Philip II of Macedon and had been taught everything he knew by the philosopher Aristotle. Alex loved the idea of passing secret messages and snooping on his own troops to see who was or wasn't pissed off. His sneaky methods must have worked, because he used them to find out who had killed his dad Philip II and later, when he decided to go a-conquering (as they all did). Starting out in 334 BC, his armies managed to crush loads of different peoples – the Triballi, the Getae, the Illyrians, the Thebans, the Persians, the Lycians, the Pisidians, the Egyptians, the Tyrians, the Ouxians, the Mardi, the Scythians, the Massagetai, not to mention all the Indians (in India). And – after lunch – the . . .

A Clever Espionage Trick

Alexander was rather fond of sending identical scrolls wrapped round staffs. He hid the secret message within a fairly ordinary boring report. The parchment was wound round and round a staff in a spiral and the message written along it in line with the staff. Unwound it made no sense whatsoever. Wrapped round a staff of identical width it could be read again. Get it? This idea was to carry on right into the twentieth century and became the blueprint for many codes on both sides. A thin strip of paper can be wrapped tightly round a pencil and the message written along the line of the pencil. When the paper's pulled out it reads as pure nonsense. Try it.

The Roman Republic (509–264 BC)

The Romans didn't create a massive empire without a large amount of undercover jiggery-pokery. Many Roman authors of the time let it be known that espionage was widespread and that the Romans had a huge network of spies resident in foreign lands. They also had double agents (called exploratores) who posed as mates of Rome's enemies while all the time sending back lots of juicy stuff about their armies and where they went and when. At home, these chaps took the form of a sort of underground police (a bit like the Gestapo in Germany), infiltrating any groups who looked as though they might be planning to attack their Emperor or his chums.

The speculatores were another bunch attached to each Roman legion as secret service operators. They even had a club called the schola speculatorum where they'd meet and swap tall stories and tricky trade secrets over a pint (of wine).

Henry II (1133–1189)

In the higher circles of espionage there is a term that is bandied about as a kind of warning to all would-be renegades even to this day. It's called 'the Henry II syndrome'. It all started with the rather serious rift between King Henry and his Archbishop of Canterbury, Thomas à Becket, way back in the 1100s. The Archbishop was becoming annoyingly fond of the way Roman Catholics and the Pope were doing things but, unfortunately, his old chum Henry most certainly wasn't. It was when the old archbish started excommunicating (chucking out of the church) lots of Henry's favourite servants that the King began to really get his royal knickers in a twist. One day Henry happened to say, almost in passing, to four of his most favoured knights, 'Who will rid me of this turbulent priest?'

and the knights, who were extremely licky and anxious to please, took him at his word. That night they went to Canterbury (where Archbishops of Canterbury usually live) and promptly set about him with their freshly sharpened swords. Unfortunately Henry hadn't meant that at all and suffered the most appalling guilt for causing the death of someone who had once been his best mate.

In modern spying circles, therefore, they use the term 'Henry II syndrome' as a warning to anyone who takes a politician, or military leader's idle comment seriously (perish the thought) or simply carries out an action on their own to gain favour. The Buster Crabb affair in the fifties (page 67) was a good example of this.

By the Way

It all turned out all right for Thomas in the end (apart from being murdered) as he was made a saint in 1173.

Blondel (Twelfth Century)

I don't know if you are aware of this but King Richard the Lionheart (the one Robin Hood made all the fuss about) was almost certainly gay – and a good job too as it turned out. Richard's best friend was a French guy called Blondel de Nesle who accompanied him all through his campaign in Palestine to thwart the mighty Saladin (head Muslim). In 1192, while rushing through Austria on his way home early from the Holy Land to sort out his naughty brother John, poor Richard was captured and held to ransom in a secret castle by the Duke of Austria (they did a lot of that sort of thing in those days).

Back home, it seemed fairly natural and appropriate for the king's loyal followers to ask Blondel if he wouldn't mind going on a spying mission to find his boss and boyfriend – but he'd have to have a disguise. We next hear of Monsieur de Nesle in heavy disguise, dressed as a travelling minstrel, admittedly looking rather soppy (bells on pointy hat and stuff), trudging all the way through Germany and into Austria, stopping outside every blinking castle to sing Richard's favourite tune (on account of Richard had composed it). He also presumably had to pretend to be German. Blow me down if he wasn't singing away gay-ly outside some old Austrian castle when he heard the faint voice of his old mate joining in with the chorus. The spying had paid off. Blondel dashed home to England, raised the £3,000,000

SOUNDS FAMILIAR

ransom that the greedy old Austrian duke had demanded and got his best friend, the king, out.

I'd like to report they lived happily ever after, but a little later Richard died while trying to get back the bit of France which he'd once owned. He was only 41. Rotten luck, really. He was hit by a bolt from the very weapon (the crossbow) that he'd introduced to France! Quel dommage!!

The Ninjas (Twelfth Century)

Would you believe it but those ludicrous half-men/half-turtles called the Ninja Turtles really existed (well, the ninja did) way back in twelfth century Japan. They were a sub-branch of the famous samurai who were probably the bravest warriors that ever lived. Back in those days there was big trouble between all the ruling families in Japan but by 1189, a chap called Yorimoto became supreme shogun – the Japanese name for a military leader (and a rather good jeep). It was he who first trained up the ninjas to go on special spying missions to find out what his enemies were up to. These horribly fit young men were trained from the age of five to hang from the branches of trees for ages (for some little remembered reason), swim underwater for long distances, walk tightropes (useful for spying on circuses), make and then operate machines to help them fly, and best of all to learn ninjitsu – the ancient art of disguises and tricks to make themselves invisible.

CAN YOU SEE ME NOW?

Genghis Khan (Twelfth Century)

The little baby who was to become the mighty Genghis Khan was born Temujin in 1167 by Lake Baikal, Russia. His dad was the ruler of all the land between the Amur River and the Great Wall of China (built to keep him and all his Mongol kind out). Temujin took over when only thirteen and had one hell of a job to keep his position, as the rest of his tribe were always revolting (in every way possible). But the young lad turned out to be a legendary leader and fierce fighter and soon had his lot and all the neighbouring tribes well under control. So under control that in 1206, these beastly barbarians all decided to make him their leader, calling him Genghis (which means 'precious warrior' in Chinese), and Khan (which means 'lord' in Turkish). Flushed with success, Genghis Khan began to look around for pastures new to conquer, for the moody Mongols needed a lot more grass on which to feed their millions of horses★.

NICE GRASS!

★*Breeding and eating horses was basically all the Mongols ever did.*

He began to wonder what exactly was over that Great Wall he'd heard about and decided to find out. So saying, in 1213, he and his horrible hordes invaded China (and presumably ate all their grass). The rest is history and not for this little book, but it must be said that Genghis Khan became known as the greatest military leader the world has ever seen.

His success not only lay in his merciless savagery, but his use of intelligence to work out the weaknesses of his enemies. One of his best wheezes was to send his most trusty scouts out to his foes claiming they were deserters and saying that they really didn't want to be Mongols any more. When these spies found out all they needed to know, they snuck back to whoever it was they'd 'deserted' from and spilled the beans.

Also Genghis asked his travelling merchants and traders to double as spies in order to keep him up to date with what went on in foreign lands. Information could be quickly relayed back to the lord and master over massive distances by a unique early postal service. This involved a rider in a special sort of Mongol postman's outfit, dashing at full pelt (upon a horse, of course) between staging points which were twelve fast galloping-hours apart and where fresh horses would be waiting. It was said that a single rider could achieve three hundred miles in a day (not to mention a very sore bum).

OH NO! HE'S COMING

By the Way
This system apparently gave the idea, centuries later, to the men who set up the Pony Express in the wild and woolly west of America.

Council of Ten (Fourteenth Century)
If you go back to the Renaissance period in the 1300s, to Venice to be precise, the Doge (chief magistrate), Marino Falieri, was found to be heading a nasty conspiracy designed to topple the sovereignty of the noblemen of the Venetian Republic. He was executed in 1355 for his trouble. To counteract this sort of unsociable behaviour, a group called the Consiglio degli Dieci (Council of Ten) was set up. These were a spooky bunch who acted as sort of official snoopers or spies controlling the secret police, espionage, and counter espionage and had almost unlimited power. They would wear sinister masks at official gatherings so's not to be recognised, but would open their long cloaks, if challenged, to flash (no jokes please) the official insignia which were woven into their linings.

By the Way
Venetian counter-intelligence agents successfully outwitted industrial spies from another Italian city, Genoa (their sworn enemies), who were trying to pinch the secret methods by which the Venetians made their internationally admired cannons.

Sir Francis Walsingham (1530–1590)
If ever there was a time when England needed a proper secret service, it was around the time of Elizabeth I. Sir Francis Walsingham was her under-secretary and soon realised that there were far too many foreign, particularly

French, chappies hanging around the dark alleys of London – probably up to no good (still are, in my humble opinion). France, by the way, was even then our very worstest enemy and had quite a well developed spy network.

First off, Walsingham got the Lord Mayor to draw up a weekly list of all foreigners arriving and leaving the city and had routine checks to see what they were up to (now there's a good idea).

Walsingham was made Ambassador to France in 1570, in an effort to cool things down between the two countries. Actually, if truth be told, it gave him a better chance to set up a network of spies in their country. Poor Francis, by the way, had to finance all these shady characters out of his own pocket, as the meanie old queenie was by then infamous for keeping the royal purse-strings tightly knotted. 'Knowledge is never too dear,' Walsingham pleaded in vain.

He eventually came home in 1573 to become the

queen's first secretary and a member of the privy council, but everyone knew that his real job was to keep a watchful eye abroad using all the new contacts he'd made.

But it was still costing him a fortune and Francis eventually went belly up financially due to having to almost single-handedly finance England's intelligence service overseas. It was a shame really, for at the time all those fearful foreigners were spending far more on theirs.

This under-financing was dangerous in other ways, for when European diplomats realised how little our poor English diplomats were actually paid, they dangled jingly bags of gold in front of them in order to gain their services, which on several occasions worked. Sir Edward Stafford for one, went over as Ambassador to France, but it was soon noticed by the Spaniards (who were planning to invade us) how short of the old loot he was. He became their agent but when found out was never brought to trial. Current theory was that dear old Eddie worked as a double-agent, certainly giving the Spaniards bits and pieces of trivial information but all the time keeping Walsingham up to date on what they were up to. Nice one!

Walsingham battled on and by 1587 managed to convince his chums (and the Queen) that the biggest threat was indeed from the Spanish (our new worstest enemy) mostly because one of his top men (a certain Richard

Gibbes) was warning him every five minutes of a massive armada (bunch) of 150 ships that had gathered over Spain way – and were, to put it mildly, all pointing this way! As cover, Gibbes had posed as a supporter of the Catholic Mary Queen of Scots who the Spanish wanted on our throne.

Walsingham stepped up his secret service to such a point that he was no longer just listening to what was going on in deepest Spain. Better than all that, he had men right in the thick of the Spanish court and even managed to influence the date for their long awaited attack on England. By twisting the arms of King Philip's bankers in Genoa, he was able to hold up the loans necessary for putting the finishing touches to their fleet (guns, sails, flags, ship's biscuits and things). The rest everyone knows. There is no doubt that one of the reasons the Spanish were thrashed so soundly was because our little fleet knew all about them and, better still, thanks to Richard Gibbes, knew exactly at what time they'd turn up (2.15 on Tuesday). It's due to the likes of these chaps that we didn't become part of the Spanish empire and you're not called something like Don Miguel or Anna Maria (apologies if you are).

Gilbert Gifford (Sixteenth Century)

He was a young Catholic languishing in gaol on a charge of fraud during the reign of Elizabeth I. When he was released he went to work for the Catholic Mary Queen of Scots (the one who Liz was convinced was trying to overthrow her) but offered himself to Walsingham as a spy in her camp. He read all her secret messages which were left in barrels and wine bottles and, best of all, was let in on the elusive code that the Pope used for all his letters and stuff. This meant that Walsingham and therefore Queen Elizabeth could second guess just about every move the enemy made, and eventually were able to uncover the Babington plot against her, which lead to the severe removal of cousin Mary's still pretty head on 8 February, 1587.

Christopher Marlowe (1564–1593)

Many people believe that Christopher Marlowe wrote quite a lot of the plays that Will Shakespeare got the credit for. He was certainly around at the same time and was certainly very good at it (playwriting that is). Marlowe was the second son of a Cambridge cobbler and went to Cambridge University in 1579. He nearly didn't get his degree because towards the end of his course he was hardly ever there (I know the feeling). Luckily, a letter turned up from the Privy Council in the nick of time saying that he'd been up in London 'on matters touching the benefit of his country'. I'll say he was. Chris, as it turned out, was in Queen Elizabeth's secret service. Sir Francis Walsingham (remember him?), as head of the Secret Service, had been employing a few of the brighter Cambridge undergraduates (always good for recruitment spies) and sending them over to Rheims in France. Rheims was a bit of a hotbed for spies and counterspies. Pretending to be a Catholic★, he got in with

★ *He was actually an atheist who seemed to delight in blasphemy.*

the Duke de Guise, a chum of the King of Spain (our enemy), and had a great time finding out the names of Catholic conspirators stationed in England.

It all went pear-shaped however, as that sort of thing so often did (and does), and the next we hear of our Chris was in 1593 when he was arrested for reasons unknown. He was released on bail but ten days later the playwright and poet was dead, killed in a pub brawl in Deptford. His killer was, surprisingly, given a free pardon, so it really doesn't take the head of MI5 to work out that the poor chap was probably murdered. Why? I bet Queen Elizabeth I might have been able to tell you.

WRITE A POEM ABOUT THAT, IF YOU CAN

Oliver Cromwell (1599–1658)

Have you ever wondered how Roundhead leader Oliver Cromwell managed to defeat King Charles I in the Civil War of 1640? Probably not. Well, I'll tell you anyway. It was largely because of his deep belief in the merits of spying. Despite the Royalists' best efforts to keep their mouths shut, the

Parliamentarians (Roundheads) seemed to end up with secrets galore, almost solely through Cromwell's head of intelligence, the first real master spy, the brilliant John Thurloe. Later, when in power, he controlled a network of listeners at doors, not only at home but throughout Europe where there were hundreds of Royalist plots to overthrow Cromwell.

Thurloe, an ex-Essex lawyer, became Home Secretary, Foreign Secretary, Secretary of State, Chief of Police, head of the Secret Service, War Secretary, Postmaster General and Councillor of States – all at the same time! – and with a budget of £70,000 purely for spying. Not bad! This meant total control, making his regime so tight that one of the Italian Council of Ten (see page 21) heard from the Venetian Ambassador that, though England seemed completely up-to-date on what everyone else was doing, practically none of their own secrets ever escaped.

Thurloe did it by flashing wads of money around the Royalists abroad and most of the foreign courts – for 'good agents,' he claimed, 'cannot be gained but by money; for money they will do anything'. Back in England he divided the country into eleven districts, each policed by his own sort of militia. They intercepted practically every letter sent and offered cash rewards to anyone who'd snitch on their neighbours.

By the Way

The only reason Ollie
Cromwell died peacefully
in his bed was
because Thurloe
was totally aware
of every single
plot to kill him.

DEAD BUT HAPPY

John Churchill (1650–1722)

Back in the seventeenth century John Churchill, otherwise known as the first Duke of Marlborough, loved espionage and spent a fortune on it. He was famous for saying in defence of its great cost, 'No war can be conducted successfully without early and good intelligence, and such advices cannot be had but at very great expense'. He was obviously remembering the battle of Sedgemoor in 1685, a typical good news and bad news scenario. The good news was that a spy told the rebel Duke of Monmouth everything he needed to know about the royal army nearby. The bad news was that he forgot to mention a devilishly deep water-filled ditch which just happened to run between the two camps. When Monmouth's army attacked in the middle of the night, the Royalist army was woken by the sound of men splashing and cursing and promptly rushed out and beat them hollow. The even worse news was that poor old Monmouth was to lose his head a few days later.

Tsar Paul

Catherine the Great's boy Paul took his mum's idea of a Secret 'Expedition' (Secret Service) one step further. He encouraged everyone in Russia to snitch on everyone else, and put a big yellow box outside his palace where anyone from a road-sweeper to a high-ranking politician could drop in secret information about someone he knew (just imagine that at school). It all got a bit out of hand and so petty that one poor officer got a one-way ticket to the freezing wastes of Siberia simply for being seen wearing his cap at the wrong angle. Anyway the whole idea backfired as Tsar Paul, obviously thinking his yellow box would at least keep him aware of plots and stuff, was assassinated in 1801 by a gang of his very own army officers. Apparently this had been the result of a huge plot of nobles and military men who were fed up with the Tsar's increasingly loopy behaviour (and presumably his blasted yellow box).

Duke of Wellington (1769–1852)

Sir Arthur Wellesley, the Iron Duke, the bloke who trounced Napoleon in 1815 (Battle of Waterloo) was a spymaster supreme and commented, 'All the business of war is to find out what you don't know by what you do.' He would send spies out to find out everything about where a battle was likely to take place, what the enemy commanders were like, how their troops were trained, and even what they got to eat and probably how often they went to the lav (Water-loo?). He would even ask foreign locals what they thought about the British.

NOT INVENTED YET – ED.

Charles Geneviève Louis August Andrè Timothèe d'Eon de Beaumont (1728–1810)

If it wasn't bad enough having a mouthful like that for a name, young d'Eon (as we'll call him for short), was brought up by his mother to wear girl's clothes till his early teens. Helped by his pretty face and slight build, the young d'Eon would slip in and out of women's clothes at will and seemed to quite enjoy it (no comment!). But, strange as it might seem, young d'Eon was no sissy. In fact, as well as having a law degree, he was reckoned to be a superb athlete and the most brilliant swordsman in all France.

He was soon noticed by King Louis XV, who had his own little spying outfit (called Le Secret de Roi), and asked to go on a strange mission. Using his ability to drop into girl's gear at the drop of a chapeau, he was sent to the court of the Tsarina Elizabeth in St Petersburg, Russia, disguised as a young lady called Mlle Lia de la Belmont. Oddly enough, the Tsarina herself liked to dress as a man. Is this all getting a bit weird? D'Eon or, should we say, Mlle Lia was asked to find out (and did) just how close the Russians and the British had got towards putting a joint army together and if possible get them to favour France instead (French diplomats had been banned from St Petersburg for years). So far so good.

It all worked a treat. The rather butch Tsarina thought the girl was fab and made her her maid of honour. All the French court painters wanted to paint the fresh new beauty in town little guessing she was really a bloke. Gradually

d'Eon, while continually sending coded messages back home, managed to change Elizabeth's mind about the French and even to halt any idea she might have of signing a deal with the British. So far so even better.

Eventually the Tsarina was told the girl's secret and luckily was tickled pink, thinking it all a right laugh (that's cross-dressers for you). She even offered our hero a high rank in the Russian Army which he/she gracefully declined.

It had all gone so brilliantly and the young man returned to France in a blaze of glory with 300 gold coins and a miniature portrait of the Tsarina herself. The French king was also delighted and presented him with a jewel-encrusted snuff-box. D'Eon was then made a permanent fixture in the French Secret Service at 3,000 livres a year. Things couldn't be better.

One of his most famous spying jobs was when he was asked to come to England (as secretary to the French Ambassador). The French planned to invade England and d'Eon's real job was to find out the best route to take once they landed (left out of Margate, right at Croydon etc.). But all was not well back home. The king's dreadful new mistress, the infamous Madame de Pompadour, had always resented Louis's Secret Service and attempted to weed out its members and destroy them. Top of the list was our d'Eon and the mean madam tried to get him to come back to France, even stopping his pay when he refused. Her men then tried everything – poisoning, kidnapping, having him banged up in an asylum – you name it, but it was all to no avail.

It was when the old King died that things really hit the skids, however. Charles was broke and needed to get home, so he wrote to the new King Louis XVI and told him that he was really a woman and that if he was anything like his dad he'd get the joke and send for him. Unfortunately the new Louis didn't – and insisted that he must never dress as a

French officer again, cos it was an insult to France. He could come home, he conceded, but he must always be seen as a woman. Hmmm, tricky.

D'Eon was forced to agree but had his fingers crossed when he promised to obey. A little later he was arrested in France for impersonating a French officer (and a man) and shipped back to London where, to qualify for an allowance, he had again to dress as a woman for life. D'Eon lost the plot completely but Londoners thought it great and there were massive bets (millions of pounds) placed on whether or not he was indeed a man or a woman.

The rest of the story is so sad that it almost doesn't bear repeating. D'Eon was forced to remain as a woman for the rest of his life till his death in a cheap lodging house in 1810. He was 83 and poverty-stricken. His landlady, undressing the withered 'old lady' for her final trip (six feet under), was suitably horrified to discover the answer to the riddle that had kept Londoners guessing for years.

Sidney Reilly b.1874

'Reckless Reilly', as he was known, was the spy to end all spies – the man who could have outwitted and out-womanised James Bond with both hands (and everything else) tied behind his back. He even looked a bit like the American film star Humphrey Bogart. Reilly was actually born in Odessa, Russia, in 1874, not Ireland (as he claimed) and his real dad had been a Jewish doctor in Vienna, not a Russian army colonel. This made him not Sidney Reilly but Sigmund Georgievich Rosenblum. Being Jewish in anti-Semitic Russia was, as you can imagine, a bit of a no-no, so young Sidney, Sigmund, or whatever you want to call him, decided to run for it. Sly Sid soon became the best kind of adventurer, popping up all over the world, using the many languages he spoke fluently. He even became one time in the early 1890s, the cook on the British expeditionary party that went up the Brazilian Amazon – no mean feat in those days. It was on this particular outing that its leader, the well-known spymaster, Major Fothergill, noticed Sidney's many qualities and offered him a job in the British Secret Service.

So, in 1896, our Sidney became a proper secret agent (a double-agent even) working in the Far East for the British and the Japanese both at the same time (really Reilly!!).

By the Way

Sydney Reilly took his name (Reilly) from a wealthy widow called Margaret Reilly Thomas whose husband, the Reverend Hugh Thomas, he kindly helped murder at the end of the century.

Later, in 1906, he turned up apparently working for the Russian Tsar, having an amazingly posh apartment in St Petersburg full of priceless old masters but all the time still a special agent for the British. Basically Reilly would search the world to see where the most trouble was going on and get amongst it, working for whoever would pay the most. He had no fear and at one time, during the First World War was parachuted behind German enemy

lines where he stayed, playing at being a perfect Hun,
gathering secret information at the infamous Krupps
weapons factory and killing two guards for good measure
when he had to leave rather smartish. For this he gained our
Military Cross for bravery.

After the war Reilly, who was obsessed with overturning
the Russian regime, particularly Lenin, travelled in and out
of Russia with a pass saying he was a member of the Soviet
Secret Police.

It all came to a sticky end (or didn't) in 1925 when he
was shot (or wasn't) trying to cross the Finnish border into
Russia, but neither the Russians nor the Brits would say
anything about it – more than likely because they didn't
know. Some say he was executed in 1925, others say they
saw him walking about, large as life, in 1927. Whether he
was shot or really died or is even alive now (aged 135) will
probably never be known. All we do know is that however
Sidney Reilly really kicked the bucket it would have to have
been just how he had lived – shrouded in deceit, double-
crossing and mystery. Whether Reilly was really working for
us or the Russians (or even the blinking Irish come to that)
is probably the biggest mystery of all. One thing is for
certain, Sidney Sigmund Georgievich Rosenblum Reilly
was the most celebrated spy of all time and he alone laid the
foundation stone for the spy ring that eventually wriggled
right into the heart of British society.

The Boy Scouts

Did you know that Lord Baden-Powell, the chap who
founded the Boy Scouts in 1908, was once a spy? Better
still, did you know that Himmler, who was the head of the
Gestapo (Germany's secret police) during the Second World
War, actually reckoned that because of this the Scouts had to

be a branch of the Secret Service? I wonder what he thought the Guides and Brownies were up to?

Baden-Powell was a bit of a whiz with the old paintbrush and while sketching butterflies, would integrate outlines of enemy fortifications or weapons into the complicated wing patterns and send them home. Another trick was to soak his clothes in strong booze and totter off towards secret German military installations. Having had a good snoop around he'd usually be found but, because they reckoned a complete drunk was no threat to anyone, the sentries would kick him out.

UNLIKELY SPIES

Prime Suspect

Can you imagine anywhere more innocent-sounding than Laburnum Cottage, Pittville Crescent Lane, Cheltenham? This was the home of Mr Geoffrey Prime, a highly respectable rep for a wine company, and his wife. Little did the neighbours know of the real Mr Prime.

On 27 April 1982, a couple of policemen called at the Primes' front door and asked if Mr Prime owned a two-tone, brown and cream Ford Cortina (a crime in itself). They were trying to find out why it had been seen in the same location as a series of assaults on young girls over the last couple of years. Prime denied knowing anything about it, but after they'd gone, broke down and confessed to his wife that he had committed the assaults. The good lady said she would support him through all the trials and tribulations ahead. Imagine her surprise however, when having got all that off his chest, her hubby threw caution to the wind and went on to confess to having been a Russian spy for the last fourteen years. I suppose he must have thought that having confessed to being a right old perv, a spy wouldn't seem so bad.

The next day Prime went to the police and told all . . . well almost all – he somehow forgot to mention the spying bit. The shocked Mrs Prime, waiting patiently at home, still didn't believe her old man had been a spy until she peeked into his briefcase (still on the hall table) and found, under a false bottom, a full spying kit – right down to a miniature camera, invisible writing equipment and a load of special little codebooks. After asking the advice of her priest, solicitor and doctor (why not the milkman? I ask) she decided to spill the beans to the cops. Even the officer in

charge didn't believe that the rather dorky looking Prime could possibly have been such a dark and mysterious figure, but when he saw the old miniature spy outfit he immediately rang Special Branch who were round before he'd even put the phone down.

On further investigation they found that Prime wasn't just a little man sending the odd piece of not very important stuff to the Russians, but a big deal main agent dealing in the sort of secrets that made their eyes water.

Why Had he Dunnit?

Prime had been an unhappy loner as a kid and had been assaulted by an adult when very young. When he did his National Service (compulsory military training) at 18 he was found to be rather good at languages, if not much else. Prime chose Russian and, although turning out to be not as good as they at first thought, he did end up snooping on Russian voice transmissions at RAF Gatow – West Berlin.

He was then promoted to sergeant.

When arrested for spying, Prime said that he'd gone over to the Russians of his own accord, but it later looked much more probable that the Russkies had somehow discovered his more than unhealthy interest in young girls and blackmailed him into telling them how much the Brits knew of their operations and which codes they had already cracked. Prime did this so well and it pleased the Russians so much that he was sent to a special spy school at KGB headquarters in East Berlin where he was given a complete spy kit and, of course, money. It was all a bit of a laugh really for, while Prime was being vetted for an incredibly important security job in England (which he passed with flying colours), he was actually away learning how to spy on them. What a cad!

In his new English job Geoffrey Prime was supposed to continue to listen in on top secret Russian technical conversations and report to British Intelligence what they were saying. What he actually did was tell the Russians which of their lines of communication he was tapping so that they could pass a load of inaccurate hogwash to anyone listening. All this was in 1969 and Prime went on spying for years despite being intensively vetted six times by British Intelligence (scary or what?). He was so convincing that in 1975 he was promoted again (by us lot) and found himself working amongst top secret material that came over by satellite from the CIA in America.

When eventually the KGB decided that Prime was of no

further use, they cunningly decided to throw him to the wolves by wining and dining him in public with well-known Soviet agents at top Viennese restaurants. This was done purely so that the British agents known to use the same places would spot them, and then Prime, and then deal with him in the usual way. But although the Russkies flaunted him around all the flashest hotels and restaurants, they weren't spotted once by the British agents (Lord help us). Prime carried on for another two years before being arrested, as we now know, on a pure fluke. The man that Special Branch originally thought was a sad, inadequate pervert turned out to be a frightfully clever and important Russian agent who during his time removed, photographed and passed on countless top secret documents.

Geoffrey Prime was sentenced to 35 years for spying and a further three for indecent assault on children. He is presumably still in Long Lartin prison to this day (and, if our intelligence services have anything to do with it, still communicating with the Russians).

Sir Anthony Blunt

Here is the headline news from 20 November, 1979.

A shocked House of Commons heard today that the Queen's

distinguished art adviser and friend, Sir Anthony Blunt, 72, is a Russian spy. He was the notorious fourth man in the famous Burgess, Maclean and Philby affair whom all the secret services had been trying to track down for years. Sir Anthony will, of course, be immediately stripped of his knighthood.

This was the final link in a story that had intrigued the world of espionage for years. It all began back in 1926 at Cambridge University when the young, gawky, idealistic, but nonetheless brilliant, vicar's son (not to mention relative of the Queen Mother) was made a tutor as soon as he'd finished his studies. At that time a lot of the posh Cambridge undergrads were carried away with the idea that Britain and the west were sliding further into the hideous world of Capitalism (which we did – thank God) and were hell-bent on making us follow the bleak path of Communist Russia. Blunt was the first recruited by the Russkies in 1933 and his first convert (and lover, as it turned out) was Guy Burgess who, with Blunt, became one of the 'Ring of Five', perhaps the most famous spy ring ever organised by the KGB. Their first job was to help the Russians stop the Nazis who were making nasty noises over in Germany. They in turn recruited Donald Maclean, the lesser-known American, Michael Straight, and lastly Kim Philby. Blunt's main job became to spot anyone else amongst the undergrads who might want to do the same sort of thing (and cheat on their country at the same time).

By the Way

In case you might be thinking that this all sounds very 'Cambridge' and gentlemanly, it might interest you to note that Blunt was not above blackmailing his lads by threatening to reveal their homosexuality (at that time illegal) to the cops.

It was totally bizarre that Blunt was accepted by MI5 in 1939 at the beginning of the war, especially when you consider that he was a fully paid-up Marxist in earlier life. But accepted he was, and he proceeded to wreck MI6's counter-espionage efforts abroad without anyone having a clue what he was up to. He also let his Russian bosses know exactly who was sending secrets to Britain, and gave them names and addresses of everyone who worked for MI5. When he was put in charge of surveillance (spy watching) he was finally able to tell his Soviet bosses exactly who was watching who, where and when, whichever side they were on. Anthony Blunt was actually the perfect spy.

All through this period Blunt had managed to keep his job as deputy director of the dead flash Courtauld Institute of Art and even met his spy mates in his office at Portman Square, using the office's equipment to copy important documents which were then sent on to Moscow. A lot of the stuff he sent at the time, regarding the exact location of the soon-to-be-happening Normandy landings would have cost thousands of Allied lives had his Russian bosses acted on it.

Blunt left MI5 after the war to be the incredibly important Surveyor of Pictures for George VI. This provided fab cover for his other new job as messenger boy for Russian spies, at the same time giving them any information he could wheedle out of his old colleagues in MI5. Things eventually became a bit hot for Blunt when his old college chums Burgess and Maclean did a runner to Russia but he refused to go himself, purely because working for Buckingham Palace was such a doddle. Despite being interrogated by the British intelligence services practically every five minutes, (they were sure he must be up to something) he continued to pass messages to and fro for years.

In 1963 the game was suddenly up when a former Soviet spy working oddly enough as President Kennedy's art adviser in the States, suddenly confessed all and named Blunt as the agent who'd recruited him. Amazingly, Blunt was told that if he spilled all the beans, naming names and explaining codes, he wouldn't be prosecuted. Odd that. Anyone else would have been severely executed for high treason. It is now thought that it was only his high-up royal connections that saved him. For whatever reasons, it appears that Blunt did confess all. Or did he?

It now looks like all the information he gave under oath was a pack of lies designed purely to throw the British off the real track. Either way, his lurid career seemed to have been soon forgotten and years later he was even knighted for work carried out for – wait for it – MI5! It is now thought that the 'work' he did was to whip over to Berlin to retrieve records of a very embarrassing liaison between our dead dodgy Duke of Windsor (a closet Nazi) and a certain gentleman called Adolf Hitler.

In 1983 a book came out telling the whole sorry story of Burgess, Maclean and, much more to the point, Blunt. This time the game was up good and proper and the country was baying for his traitorous blood. Blunt, aged 76, died broken and alone in 1983, a disgrace to all who knew him.

Ian Fleming

You'd never think that the guy who created James Bond knew a lot about real espionage, would you? You'd be wrong. Not only did Ian Fleming (1908-1964) know a lot about it, he'd been in it up to his suave and sophisticated neck for most of his working life – before deciding to write. Not only that, but you might be forgiven for thinking he was a bit like our Mr Bond himself.

Son of wealthy parents, a playboy around London and bored with life as a stockbroker, young Ian craved excitement. He eventually met someone in British Naval Intelligence who was looking for bright young guys who, feeling they had nothing to lose, were prepared to do just about anything as long as it was dangerous and the money good. Fleming was perfect – mad as a hatter, brave as a bulldog – and with ideas galore.

Fleming's first solo job during the Second World War, was for Room 39 (as his department was nicknamed) and involved the famous Rudolf Hess (Hitler's deputy leader of the German National Socialists). He reckoned that if he could get one of the Nazis' top men to defect to us, it would strike pure fear into the Germans. He chose the infamous Hess purely because of his one weakness. He was deeply into astrology (star signs) and therefore could be led to believe almost anything★. Fleming managed to get at the two Swiss astrologers known to be used by high-ranking

★*In my opinion.*

German officers and told them to tell Hess that his big moment of truth was nigh, and it was him who had been chosen by the fickle finger of fate to go to England and smoke big pipe of peace with our Prime Minister. This, without any doubt, would make him the greatest and most popular man in the whole wide world. In 1941 Hess swallowed the bait big time, borrowed a Messerschmidt fighter and flew it to Scotland where he ordered the somewhat gobsmacked local police to take him to their leader.

Oh dear, instead of being delighted, the British Government, including PM Winston Churchill, saw him as not only an embarrassment but potentially dangerous. They were worried that he might shine a torch on all the high-up Britons (including the Duke of Windsor) who'd been having cosy fireside chats with the top German, Hitler. The government therefore let it be known that Hess was, as near as dammit, a total loony and no use to man nor beast. Hess went to jail and stayed there till he died in 1989.

By the Way

Hitler went crazy when the story got out and every single clairvoyant, astrologer or fortune teller was arrested and their craft, art, or whatever you might jokingly call it, banned (even Hitler showed some sense).

YOU'RE GOING ON A LONG JOURNEY - TO JAIL

James Bond – sorry – Ian Fleming (code name 17F) was a proper spy. He broke into safes in foreign consulates, photographed secret documents, made plasticine casts of keys, stole never-seen-before enemy aircraft engines and even kidnapped the first German one-man submarine, complete with dead driver. After the war he promised a friend that he'd write 'the spy story to end all spy stories'. And didn't he do well!

The Real James Bond

Everyone's heard of James Bond, in fact some people would find it difficult to name another spy. But did anyone like him really exist? Legend has it that he was just a huge mish-mash of all the agents Ian Fleming had ever met – with a great dollop of idealism thrown in. 'M' on the other hand, was really a chap called Maxwell Knight, one time boss of MI5 and a brilliant spy catcher. Fleming got the idea of the one letter name from a chap called Vernon Kell – codename 'Major K'.

The British Secret Services were born in 1909 and Bond's fore-runners would have been a three-officer outfit. Their back up team would have consisted of a secretary, a cleaning lady and just a simple motto: 'Trust no one.' Since the 1914 war the number of agents rose to 10. But however amateur our lot had been, the German agents were even worse. Practically all their devices and tricks were known by the British.

The dashing, devil-may-care, one-man hit squad that was James Bond did not exist, nor did anyone remotely like him. Apart from anything else, if his hazardous life style hadn't killed him, his self-indulgence would. It's been calculated that he'd have slept with over 70 women a year, smoked 70 unfiltered black Russian cigarettes a day and drunk enough martinis (shaken not stirred) to kill a bar full of Irishmen. He was licensed to kill all right – himself!!

The Krogers

When I was a kid I sometimes used to ride my bike down Cranley Drive in the leafy, dare I say rather boring, suburb of Ruislip, as it was very near where I was brung up. I must have passed number 45, and it must have been when Mr and Mrs Kroger lived there. So what, I hear you cry? Well, I'll tell you so what! The Krogers turned out to be a couple of the most famous Russian spies ever to live in England, and 45 Cranley Drive became the headquarters of one of the most infamous communist spy rings run by one of the Soviet's cleverest agents. But why Ruislip? Easy! Because nothing has

ME

ever happened there before or since. Brilliant!

Back to the plot.

Nobody had noticed the rather smart, good-looking chap with the small briefcase who visited the dull-as-dishwater Krogers every few weeks for supper. He was ...

Konon Trofimovich Molody (alias Gordon Lonsdale)

Comrade Molody was a famous Russian war hero who could speak practically every language backwards. When 33 he was asked to spy on Britain – a great honour. His controllers wanted to know all about British and American airbases (by the way, did I forget to mention there was a huge American base at West Ruislip?).

In 1955, disguised as a Canadian businessman and carrying the passport of a certain Gordon Lonsdale, a chap who'd gone missing (probably murdered) in Finland, Konon Molody arrived in Britain. Lonsdale/Molody set up several lucrative businesses including supplying stuff like jukeboxes and bubblegum machines to places like airbases (funny that) and even invented a car burglar alarm that won him the coveted Gold Medal at the Brussels International Trade Fair for the best British entry. With all that and the money he received from the Russians he was soon spending cash like it was going out of fashion, which tended to make one rather popular in the 50s (or any time come to that). It didn't take long before the very best people began to appear at his ritzy, no-expense-spared parties. Under the cover of his businesses, the suave, handsome company director travelled the country, but his real purpose was to make friends with anyone who had anything to do with weapons or intelligence organisations.

It was in this way that Lonsdale met the Krogers, Soviet

agents who'd fled from the States when they were about to be uncovered. In their house at Cranley Gardens they had a full set of spying equipment right down to a radio which could connect with anywhere in the world. Lonsdale used them to send all his snippets of information back home to the old country. This all went along just fine until Lonsdale met Harry Houghton – then it went even finer. OK, Houghton was only a lowly clerk, but it was where he was a clerk that was important. He worked at the top secret Admiralty Underwater Weapons Establishment at Portland, Dorset. The KGB had dug around and found out that the otherwise rather colourless clerk had been a bit of a bad boy in early life, selling stuff on the black market during the war. Small stuff, admittedly, but enough to make him highly corruptible or at least blackmailable.

Lonsdale, now calling himself Commander Alex Johnson from the US Embassy, soon discovered that Houghton would do practically anything for money especially if it was for untraceable cash and, with his middle-aged girlfriend Bunty Gee, was tricked into believing that he was getting all the secret stuff for our American allies. Soon the most classified top secret information about our navy and docks was winging its way over the airwaves from Cranley Drive – not to America but to Moscow.

Eventually Houghton and Bunty's lifestyle gave them away. How could a man on £714 a year afford a flash new car and an expensive new house, let alone the lifestyle to go with it? MI5 put them under surveillance and were able to watch all the swapping-of-bags-in-public-places routine between them and Lonsdale.

So now Lonsdale was on the hook and he led his shadows to his bank where he casually deposited a small brown case which was found to contain a miniature Russian camera, a magnifying glass (so's he could see the camera?) and a load of assorted keys.

From then on it was easy. Lonsdale soon showed the British agents the way to Ruislip but, cleverly, they didn't swoop immediately. They were after the big catch. It came on 7 January, 1961, three months later. Houghton and Bunty Gee, under full surveillance, arrived at Victoria Station carrying a large shopping-bag. There they met Lonsdale and, as they swapped bags, detectives from Special Branch swooped. The bag contained four top secret files and over 300 photos of plans of Britain's ever-so-secret nuclear submarines.

Then it was back to Ruislip and the Krogers, who at first denied everything ... until even the most simple search revealed an Aladdin's cave of spying equipment and best (or worst) of all, under the floorboards, a device for sending coded messages at a rate of 200 words a minute. They were caught red-handed, and so was Lonsdale, and so was Houghton and so was Bunty Gee.

What Happened to Them All?

Lonsdale got twenty-five years gaol, but on receiving the sentence laughed out loud, as he knew that in no time he would be swapped for one of our imprisoned agents in Russia – which he was. Houghton and Gee got fifteen years each and the Krogers twenty.

The Undercover Pope

Giovanni Montini was a very ambitious lad. He entered the Catholic Church in 1920 and soon had his eye on the top job – Pope. The super-keen young novice turned out to be an absolute whiz at organisation and it was no surprise that, by 1937, he'd reached dizzy heights in the Vatican (Holy City) and was hobnobbing with your actual Pope Pius XII. The Vatican, by the way, was to have an important role during the Second World War, acting as a sort of go-between for all the different countries involved.

Anyway, Montini soon had his fingers in absolutely everything and was nicknamed 'the man who knows all and sees all'. He did indeed know everyone from diplomats to businessmen to politicians which meant that, if anyone wanted to have words with the Vatican, they had to go through our Giovanni – no messing! By the time he'd made bishop he'd become the only choice to set up the newfangled Vatican Information Service – a polite term for

an undercover intelligence agency. But when the Second World War began, Montini refused to take sides and gave away none of the secrets he knew to either side.

Enter James Jesus Angleton, the 27-year-old head of counter-espionage for the Italian government. This chain-smoking, ferret-faced Yale graduate knocked on Montini's door asking about an undercover agent, codename VESSEL, who seemed to be getting amazing information out of the highly secretive Vatican and was passing it on to the Americans. Angleton wondered if all this stuff was true or was it some load of old tosh supplied by the Russkies or the Japs, in order to deceive our side? The Americans were sure it was OK, however, and had refused to question it.

Montini the mole (see page 51) soon put him right, saying that the information was twaddle and nothing to do with what was discussed at top Vatican meetings. But there still remained the questions of who was doing it, why he was doing it and who he was working for.

It turned out that there was just one guy behind the whole silly business. VESSEL turned out to be Virgilio Scattolini, a fat little journalist and ex-pornographer who, having seen the Catholic light, packed up his seedy profession and ended up writing for the Vatican's own newspaper. When the editor found out exactly what Scattolini had been up to before joining his paper he fired him. This miffed Scattolini a great deal, so he simply carried on selling his own made-up Vatican 'secrets' from outside the Vatican walls.

Well, that is until Angleton and Montini stopped him.

The two men were suddenly pitched into the spotlight. Together they used their skills to organise the surrender of all the Germans and Italians in Northern Italy saving thousands of lives and the country from total destruction.

As for Giovanni, he went on to become Archbishop of Milan and in 1963 the sneaky, undercover wheeler-dealer became Pope Paul VI. He died in 1978 but his promotion might not have even stopped there, as there is now talk about making him a saint – which is about as far as you can get, apart from being God himself (or herself).

Les Brown – Who?

In July 1983, helicopters and ships spent a long weary night trying to locate a lonely SOS bleep. In France, radar operators did slightly better and managed to pin the signal down to Scotland, to the Firth of Clyde to be more precise. The Faslane nuclear submarine base did much better and finally homed in on – wait for it – a humble house on an estate at Erskine, near Glasgow. Fisherman Les Brown, soundly asleep in bed with his wife, had left a radio distress beacon on top of the wardrobe. The device was apparently faulty and still giving out a weak signal. The £20,000 air and sea hunt ended with poor Les being woken by a helicopter pilot and a policeman hammering on his front door.

No great harm done you might think. Unfortunately, the signal had been picked up first by a Russian spy satellite and its ability to isolate such a tiny object shocked the Russky-watchers in the West. If they could make out that, what else could they see? Not that the West had anything to complain about as it turned out. Only a few weeks later a couple of Russian jets caused an international incident by shooting down a perfectly innocent Korean airliner that had strayed into Soviet air space. They would have got away with the disaster had not the Americans been watching their every move on their own highly sophisticated surveillance satellites.

LADY SPIES

Despite Russia's Richard Sorge, a famous spymaster, saying that ladies would always be 'unfit for espionage work', spying has always been one of the only professions with equal opportunities for women. This is probably because they are generally regarded as more trustworthy than us men (please debate?). Here are a few of the most famous:

Aphra Behn

Despite her rather peculiar name, Aphra Behn (1649-1689) was probably Britain's first female spy, dating back to the seventeenth century. She was married to a Dutch merchant and, because of that fact, had specialised knowledge of Holland and the Dutch (who at that time were always threatening to invade Britain).

Unfortunately, in those days, women weren't taken very seriously, so when she sent back secret messages from Antwerp claiming that the Dutch had rebuilt their navy and were simply dying to try it out, the poor lady was ignored. They should have listened, for in 1667 a bunch of Dutch fireships sailed right up the Thames to the Medway and cheekily destroyed the English fleet which was parked★ at Chatham.

Louise de la Quérouaille

The beautiful Louise was sent by Louis XIV of France to find out what we English were really thinking during negotiations for the Treaty of Dover in 1670. There were two treaties being ironed out. One (which was top secret) was all to do with Charles II agreeing to allow England to convert to Catholicism (for £200,000 and 6,000 French troops) and the other, more formal one, was all about

★*Sorry, that should be 'moored'.*

England supporting the French against the Netherlands (for which Charles would get a cool £300,000 a year). The French king chose Louise de la Quérouaille, not only because she was dead gorgeous, but because he knew she was just the kind of babe our sleazy old king really fancied. She therefore acted as bait for King Charles, who predictably swallowed the plot hook, line and sinker. He not only took her to his bed but made her the Duchess of Portsmouth, and together they even conceived one of his many children between races at Newbury. I bet you didn't know that!

Lydia Darragh

During the American Revolution of 1775, the first President of America, George Washington (the man who claimed he never told a lie), had to use the sneakiest of tactics to fight an enemy that looked as if it would blow the American forces into the middle of the next week. The British, who the Americans were trying to break away from, were at that

time the most powerful nation in the world (difficult to
believe these days). Among Washington's many stunts, he had
his troops dress up as British
soldiers, run round the back
of the enemy and attack
them from the rear (ouch!).
He also allowed false
documents to get
nicked by enemy
spies, and even
had fake forts
built simply to
fool the enemy.
Not bad for
someone who reckoned he never told fibs.

But Washington was known best of all for his gathering
of enemy intelligence and was even given a special secret
fund from the Continental Congress for that purpose alone.
Top of the spy pile was a quiet middle-class lady called Lydia
Darragh, probably the most unlikely spy ever.

Respectable Lydia Darragh lived with her respectable
husband (Mr Darragh) at 177 South Second Street, in the
respectable city of Philadelphia. Both were devout Quakers
and hated war but not, as it happened, the individual soldiers
who fought in them.

When the Redcoats (British) took over Philadelphia the
officers seized all the best houses (including the Darraghs')
for themselves. As theirs had the biggest parlour, it was
chosen for their strategy meetings which, as you might
imagine, really pissed off the peace-loving couple. The
officers little suspected the polite, butter-wouldn't-melt-in-
her-mouth, sweet-faced lady in the grey muslin ankle-length
frock and the large-brimmed hat who took their coats as

they arrived. But dear Mrs Darragh was not quite as innocent as she appeared. For months she used her fourteen-year-old son John as a courier, passing snippets of intelligence to her eldest son Charles, a lieutenant in Washington's army, camped not far away. Most of the time the information was pretty small stuff – important admittedly, but nothing to win or lose major battles . . . until one night, when the officers suggested that she and her family went to bed early. Something big was afoot and Lydia had to know about it. Listening outside the door in her curlers and stockinged feet, Mrs Darragh not only found out that the British were finally about to attack Washington's army (including her son) nearby, but just how big their army was (5,999 men) and what equipment they had (thirteen cannons etc.). The British officers then, to her horror, actually announced the night of the attack as 4 December (only two days away), which would, of course, make a complete surprise – not to mention massacre. In the morning, having cheekily received a pass from the Brits to go over enemy lines (she said she was collecting flour from the local mill), Lydia scuttled off to get this scary news off her chest. She eventually reached the American army and spilt the beans – big time – to the shocked officers.

Needless to say, when the British Redcoats marched on Washington's camp, the Americans were so ready for them that the Brits didn't even bother to take the attack any further and turned round and scarpered.

Nobody was ever to suspect Lydia or her family and it was never mentioned officially, or in any war reports. American history, however, now hails Lydia Darragh as a true heroine whose bravery contributed to the successful struggle for American independence from Britain. Hip, hip ...

Emma Edmunds

Some women get so caught up in causes that they actually enlist in armies as men, chopping off their hair and binding their boobs so's not to stand out (if you see what I mean). Such a person was Sarah Emma Edmunds, who enlisted in the 2nd Michigan Infantry as Franklin Thompson in the American Civil War of 1861.

Daughter of a grumpy Canadian potato farmer, Emma was born in 1839 and never went to school owing to having to labour (picking grumpy Canadian potatoes) in the fields. When she was 18 her dad announced he'd chosen a husband for her. She promptly dressed from head to toe as a man and headed off. I guess she didn't go a bundle on her dad's choice. When next we hear of Emma she'd set up business, rather successfully as it happened, as a travelling Bible sales'man'. Emma's wanderings brought her back to visit her old home town, where only the family dog (name unknown) recognised her, but, glad to say, didn't snitch.

SHHH!

HE SMELLS FAMILIAR

It was around this time that Miss Edmunds (still dressed as a man) had a room in the house of a Methodist minister who headed the Flint Union Greys, the local militia. It was he who suggested that 'Franklin Thompson' (as she now called herself) joined the battalion when the Civil War broke out in 1861.

After leaving the army Emma wrote of her adventures in a book called Nurse and Spy in the Union Army in which she'd tended the sick and been a courier carrying messages to and fro on the battlefield. She's remembered, however, for the 'spy' bit of the title.

To do this she exchanged her uniform for the plantation style of a black American slave (regarded as the lowest form of life and practically invisible). She cropped her hair real close, and then, with a bottle of silver nitrate, stained her head, face, hands and feet 'as black as any African'.

She was so convincing that she was able to pass through the rebel lines without being given a second glance (at that time 3,000,000 Confederates were dark-skinned) and joined up with a bunch of slaves who were delivering coffee and grub to the troops. Even these black people didn't smell a rat (or a white girl).

Emma was then singled out and shoved into a work-gang building fortifications amongst the army of black male slaves. After her torturingly hard day's work she would stroll around the Confederate base making notes and tucking them into the soles of her shoes. After many adventures, she escaped back to the Unionists and was taken straightway to General McLellan's headquarters to tell him what she'd found out. Emma eventually returned to her home, changed into a girl again and married the boy, Linus, who had first lent her his clothes.

Later, in 1884, a rather chubby, middle-aged woman

applied for an army pension. At first they couldn't get it into their heads that she was the very same Franklin Thompson, but Emma was eventually believed and awarded a pension 'for her sacrifices in the line of duty, her splendid record as a soldier, her unblemished character and disabilities incurred in the service.' The mind boggles at the thought of what disabilities she could have incurred – and how!!

Mata Hari

Margaretha Geertruida Zelle (1876-1917) was the daughter of a rich, Dutch, and reportedly bad-tempered hatter, who during the First World War became the most famous, the most mysterious and the most sexy lady spy in history. She began her career as Lady McLeod, a cross between a belly-dancer and a common or garden stripper. She'd taken her name from her husband Captain Rudolph McLeod, a mean drunk from whom she'd separated just before reaching Paris in 1905 (aged 26). There she told everyone that her name was Mata Hari ('eye of the morning') and that she was the product of an Indian holy man and a temple dancer who'd died at birth (Mata's birth of course). Miss Hari was to become famous throughout the clubs of the city because of her willingness to dance practically nude at the drop of a hat (or anything else) and actually go home with anyone who'd pay her enough. Her best buzz, however, came in the First World War when she toured Europe sleeping with high-ranking officers on both sides, French or German, and then selling their pillow talk to their respective enemies.★

Actually, if truth be told, Mata Hari was never that beautiful (she was flat-chested with a rather large *derrière*) and the secrets weren't often much cop. I mean, who really wants to know what a German general wears in bed? But that really wasn't the point. When the French realised, in 1917, that she'd been working for both sides at once, and that neither side trusted her further than they could throw her, they arrested and tried her for treason. Her daft explanation of why one single German officer paid her 30,000 marks was the last straw. She told the court, apparently, that it was the going rate for the night. They replied by letting her know that the going rate for treason was the firing squad.

★*She was even sent to a how-to-be-a-spy school in Antwerp, by the Germans.*

Leonora Heinz

Leonora Heinz was a rather plain, rather lonely German girl who lived by herself in a smart apartment in Bonn, Germany. On March 1, 1960 she opened her front door to a good-looking young man called Heinz Suetterlin (look, I know this sounds like an ad for baked beans but bear with me). Handsome Heinz was carrying a bunch of roses and said he was answering a lonely hearts ad. Leonora told him that it must be a mistake for she'd never advertised. But – let's face it (she must've thought) – how many times had she had such an opportunity plonked right on her doorstep – and single as well! She promptly asked him in for a cup of coffee. Bad move number one, Leonora!

Suetterlin had been trained to perfection in the art of seduction by Russian spymasters who had built whole training-camps full of posh restaurants, bars and cinemas to imitate the cities of the West. Here young Russian studs (called ravens) and women (called swans or Mozhno Girls) were schooled in Western ways and particularly in how to charm the pants off important targets.

But why poor Miss Heinz? Well, surprise, surprise, she just happened to work as a secretary in the West German government's Foreign Ministry and she had been targeted purely and cynically because undercover agents had spotted just how desperate she seemed for a man. It was a well known fact that most of those extremely well-off young women employed by the West Germans and NATO had just about everything they could desire – except blokes.

Smoothy Suetterlin made Leonora Heinz fall head-over-heels in love with him, to such a degree that the poor girl had no choice when he threatened to leave her if she didn't bring home top secret documents from work. She was putty in his hands (or Heinz). Most lunchtimes, she rushed home from work to cook the lazy Suetterlin his lunch (beans on toast) while he would copy the stuff that she'd brought back in a special false-bottomed handbag (a present from Russia).

In six years she supplied over 3,000 documents, some of stupendous military importance, which were then sent on to the KGB before the ink was hardly dry. At one stage the Russians were even reading documents and messages before the German Foreign Minister himself.

The couple were eventually arrested and poor Leonora was presented with the ghastly truth that her now husband not only didn't love her, but didn't even like her – and never had. She hanged herself that very night in her cell.

DEADLY SPIES

When someone in the twilight world of espionage becomes a bit of a problem it often becomes necessary to – how shall we say? – dispense with his or her services ... permanently. This could be either because they know too much or because their services are no longer required or because they've been found working for the enemy. Most intelligence organisations have, in the past, employed proper 'hit-men', whose job is to get rid of anyone they're asked to, as quickly and as silently as possible – no questions asked. The nickname for this operation, in the spy world, is a 'wet affair'.

Here are a few of the most famous incidents throughout history (the ones that are known about, that is):

Nikolai Chochlov

Chochlov was a well known Russian spymaster who had sent loads of his lads into non-Communist Europe to get rid of so-called enemies of the state. One day in 1954 he was 'asked' to do the dirty deed himself. His target was Georgi Okolovich, a fervent Russian anti-Communist who lived in Frankfurt, Germany. It was good timing because for a long time Chochlov had been looking for a way to escape to the joys of hamburgers and Coke in America, so he decided to spare his victim and use him to get in touch with American agents. To prove he was who he was, he showed the American agents some of his special gizmos including his latest Soviet weapon, a gold cigarette case which cheekily doubled as a really nifty electric pistol, shooting deadly dum-dum bullets tastily coated in cyanide.

NO THANKS – I BELIEVE THEY'RE BAD FOR ONE

His former Russky bosses were understandably rather miffed and decided to teach him a lesson. In September 1957, Chochlov collapsed while talking at a Frankfurt meeting. He was rushed to hospital, but they couldn't find the antidote to the poison he'd obviously been given. Poor old Nikolai by this time was covered in dark brown blotches, black and blue swellings and blood was actually seeping through his skin. His hair then parted company with his head in great black tufts. Worse still, his bones began to decay and his blood started turning to water – he really wasn't a well boy at all. The doctors eventually worked out that he'd been poisoned with the drug thallium that had been exposed to atomic radiation (definitely something you don't want on your cornflakes). Poor old Chochlov miraculously survived but remained bald as an egg and covered in hideous scars.

Georgi Markov

Georgi Markov was a communist playwright who'd defected to England from Bulgaria and persisted in writing stuff that really got up the noses of the Soviet chiefs back home. One day, while waiting for a bus on Waterloo Bridge near the BBC (where he'd been working), he felt a sharp prick in his leg. He whipped round to see a man picking up an umbrella nearby. The chap said he was sorry and jumped into a taxi which sped away. Markov thought nothing of it and went home to his wife and supper. Later, while watching telly, he began to feel a bit yukky. Another four days and he was stone cold dead but none of the hospital doctors could trace what from. At the post mortem, however, they found a weeny little platinum ball embedded in his leg. It had been drilled and filled with ricin, a drug twice as powerful as cobra venom and with no known antidote. Experts now reckon it had been fired from a special miniature surgical device hidden in the umbrella's tip.

Buster Crabb

I remember this name when I was little (in 1956) because his disappearance caused massive headlines throughout the western world. Nicolai Bulganin and Nikita Krushchev, the mighty Soviet leaders, had arrived in England in their cruiser Ordzhonikidze to try, once and for all, to calm down the Cold War between the East and West, which was showing all signs of heating up and turning into a proper hot one. They warned the British to keep away from their boat – the very latest in Russian warships – which bristled with secret weapons and everything. Even our new prime minister, Sir Anthony Eden, told MI5 and MI6 to keep well away from the ship and the two Russkies. But Naval Intelligence simply didn't believe that was what he really wanted and, anyway, they couldn't bear having such a prize in their waters without being able to have a nose around. They were sure Eden would actually be delighted if they found out a lot of secret stuff about the flash Russian boat. They promptly set up radar on the cliffs of Dover so as to keep an eye on it and even made sure that Bulganin and Krushchev's rooms in Claridges Hotel were fully bugged. Better still, they went for top war hero and experienced frogman Commander 'Buster' Crabb's idea to dive under the ship's hull to have a good poke about.

Heads You Lose

After the first proper dive, poor Buster, a short, hairy, thickset man, was never seen again. Or was he? Some witnesses reported that they'd seen a group of Soviet frogmen wrestling with a lone frogman before dragging him onto their ship. A year later, however, a headless, handless body wearing the same sort of frogman's outfit as Crabb's was found nearby and identified by Crabb's widow as the man himself (I suppose she should have known – head, hands or not). Case closed? Not quite. As soon as the news hit the headlines, however, a Russian sailor reported that the Russkies had nabbed Crabb and that he was safe and sound (complete with all his bits) in a Russian jail.

Then the Russian government claimed that Crabb had actually gone over to their side of his own free will and produced a remarkably convincing snap of him dressed as a Russian sailor.

The real story will probably never be known but it is now thought that Russian spies had got wind of Crabb's plan to snoop around their precious warship and were down there waiting for him in a special little underwater compartment. They had probably dealt with him there and then in the way they knew best, so it looks like he lost his head after all. Either way the British government ended up with oodles of egg on their, as it turned out, maybe innocent faces.

TOOLS OF THE TRADE

Let's for one minute suppose you're a proper spy. For all I know, you might be (the oddest people read my books). If you are one don't bother to read this chapter, you should know it all. If you're not, but plan to be one – one day – you might need to know what sort of things you would need to Carry On Spying. Here are a few of the absolute essentials.

Pigeons

Most people only think of racing pigeons living in sheds in back gardens 'oop north' but the clever birds have been used to send secret messages as far back as Roman times (they even used swallows when they were in a bit of a hurry).

Before World War I, in this country, however, they didn't really go for pigeons as a method of passing messages, but Naval Intelligence thought otherwise and used them extensively when they couldn't get the wireless to work. The Brits even had a Field Intelligence Division which used high-flying reconnaissance balloons, each carrying a couple of pigeons, to relay information back quickly. Right up to the end of World War II, in fact, we called on a 'pigeon post' if no other method was available.

On 30 July 1942 the RSPCA gave a special award to a bird called Mercury for a special record-breaking flight. The daring dickie flew 480 miles, without stopping for breakfast, lunch or supper, all the

WHY CAN'T THEY USE THE BLASTED PHONE?

way across enemy lands and over the bleak North Sea, with an important message from a Danish resistance group tied to his leg. Over a hundred British birds had been parachuted in crates but old Mercury was the only one to return. I reckon the rest must have defected and their descendants are probably now living in complete luxury in Germany.

Invisible Ink

All spies have to pass messages between each other and it's probably better that other people don't read them. Invisible ink provides one of the easiest methods and there are many ways of making it. One of the best and simplest methods is to mix a little alum (aluminium sulphate) with water. You can then write using a pointed stick or an old fashioned dip pen. When it dries you can see nothing (apart from the paper, of course). Should you run a hot iron over it, however, the message will be revealed loud and clear. The trouble is that anyone opening an envelope to find a piece of paper with absolutely nothing on it might just smell a rat. The answer is simple. I reckon you could write a second message in pencil over the invisible one and tell your fellow conspirator to rub it out before ironing the paper. By the way, the pencil message could be your first go at 'disinformation' (see Spy Talk).

By the Way

If you think my method wouldn't work, listen to this.

Whenever Germans were captured, their captors were always puzzled by the number of lemons they were carrying. It was later discovered that they wrote messages in lemon juice over the normal ink ones.

By Another Way

The better-equipped German spies soaked their ties and socks with chemicals to be used later for invisible ink. When they got to their digs in Britain, they'd squeeze them in distilled water and, hey presto, they were ready to write.

A World of Gadgets

Size is everything (as the actress said to the bish - spy) ... the smaller the better in this case. Ian Fleming (the guy who invented James Bond), for instance, was ever so fond of a little cyanide gun disguised as a fountain pen. Others prefer dummy cigarette packets that kill you (slightly more quickly than the usual contents) by firing poison darts. Also on your shopping list could be a watch that tells you exactly where you are in the world, or shoes that have deadly retractable needles etc. etc. But most important of all gadgets to any proper spy are bugs – not the creepy-crawly kind, but weeny electronic listening devices planted somewhere in the enemy camp and designed to relay every word.

Bugs Abounding

Probably the biggest bugging operation ever, cropped up in 1968 when the Americans and the Russians agreed to build embassies in each other's countries. This was a nice friendly idea but potentially a little dodgy. The Russkies, suspicious as ever, employed one security expert to every two workers while building theirs in New York, while the far more trusting Americans in Moscow just let the Russians get on with it. Surprise, surprise, when they came to examine the finished building, they found more bugs than in a tramp's trousers – the place was riddled with 'em. Tiny microphones were actually mixed into the very concrete that built the walls – so much so that they were impossible to get rid of without pulling the whole blinking place to bits. The Yanks, never ones to be caught out, simply built three more floors on the top of the building at a cost of $40,000,000. Job done? Well er . . . perhaps not. The architect they eventually chose turned out to be no less than a Russian spy. Whoops!

Codes and Ciphers

Secret codes go back donkey's years. Jewish religious writers sometimes hid what they were saying by reversing the alphabet (using the last letter of the alphabet instead of the first and so on). Spartan generals went in for the old parchment round the staff trick (as described on page 14), while Greek writer Polybius invented the 5x5 square pic which is the basis of so many cryptographic (code) systems. Julius Caesar simple advanced each letter of the alphabet five places, now called 'The Caesar Shift' (which admittedly sounds a bit like a dance).

Although it is believed that there is no such thing as an uncrackable code, the very best ones take so long to unravel that by the time they are, they are usually of no use. The

Chinese, being dead clever, have always relied heavily on memory for their secret messages, tending to keep actual coding to a minimum. This actually has more to do with their ludicrously complicated writing system than anything else. Lately, however, they've taken to using Western alphabets – particularly Roman.

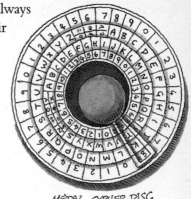

METAL CYPHER DISC
1802

In the West, the use of codes and ciphers in spy circles is as popular today as it was right back in the Middle Ages. Up till the First World War the most popular codes were usually 'substitution' ciphers. Briefly, cracking them involved comparing how often certain letters turned up in a hidden message compared to how often they'd turn up naturally in a particular language. Although somewhat difficult to work out in those days, a fairly ordinary computer could sort 'em out in minutes. This is why our decoding centre at GCHQ Cheltenham has the most extensive computer system in Europe – and that's something we're not going to share with the EEC, unless we're bonkers!

One of the great breakthroughs in coding cropped up in 1976 when Adi Shamir, an Israeli mathematician, invented a way of writing to his mate Leonard Aldeman at the University of Southern California that only he could possibly understand. I won't attempt to explain it (on account of I can't understand it), but it involved the use of large prime numbers (those numbers that can only be divided by themselves and the number one). By a system of multiplication, a set of numbers could be achieved which could only be deciphered by someone who already knew certain secret prime numbers. Clear? It is thought that even the most clever computer in the world could take years to work the code out. Even if it did, it would only take a couple of hours for the cunning codesters to put the poor machine right back where it started.

Enigma

The Germans in World War II might have been horrid, but they were ever so clever (and had the best uniforms). They invented a dead smart piece of kit called the Enigma Cryptograph, a compact machine that, despite looking a bit like a cross between a shoe box and an old fashioned cash register, scrambled messages until they read like pure gobbledegook – or, worse – German gobbledegook. There were over 150 million, million, million different settings and these were changed practically every day. The codes they spewed out were so complex that only a sister Enigma machine could understand what the hell they were talking about. A brilliant team of British codebreakers worked day and night for ages to crack its funny Kraut talk but to no avail. It was only when an actual Enigma machine was nicked and smuggled back to Britain (with an instruction book showing all the settings) that we were able to work out what they were up to. This factor alone was reckoned to have shortened the war by a good few years. When, however, the nasty Nazis realised that we were on to them, they changed all the blasted settings (typical!) and it took another huge team of top mathematicians and puzzlers (at the newly set up Government Code and Cypher School) a whole year to crack the pesky codes again.

Stop Press

On April 2, 2000, a priceless Enigma machine from the Second World War was stolen from the museum at Bletchley Park where the code-breaking team had worked. I don't suppose it can be the same person who nicked it off the Germans – he'd be in his eighties. If it is him, he's probably trying to sell it back to them. It seems rather ironic that a building that has been so involved with national security has only now begun to install its own security system.

By the Way

In an act of what looked like pure kindness, after the war Britain and America sold off their old reconditioned Enigma machines to smaller countries at silly prices, urging them to use them for their most secret communications. How thoughtful of us? Not a bit of it. All this meant was that we and the Yanks could decode all their most private communications for years to come. Does that make us clever or them stupid . . . or both?

No More Fibs

The lie detector or, to give it its proper name, polygraph has long been part of the paraphernalia used in the murky world of espionage. It's a tricky little gizmo involving four long, thin pens wired up to electronic sensors measuring pulse, breathing and even sweating. One belt goes round the victim's waist, one round the wrist, and tiny electrodes are attached to the fingers to measure moisture (sweat to you). When switched on, the pens trace thin lines around a revolving disk of graph paper. The theory is that when

someone tells a porkie, the operator is supposed to be able to see erratic up and down movements on the paper. Unfortunately, we in Britain won't have it in the house, regarding the machine about as accurate as tossing a coin and being really no more than an excitement detector. Not only that, but even if you could have detected a slight difference when someone was answering a delicate question (implying that they were fibbing) it was suspected by British Intelligence that the Soviets had a school which taught their agents methods of fooling the machine. This would become particularly useful if a spy wanted to pass on false information. As you will probably realise, the whole point of a lie detector would be missing.

By the Way

The UK, despite changing its policy and dishing out £24,000 on six brand new super-duper American lie detectors to test civil servants in crucial jobs, threw them all away in 1985. Not only, I must add, because they didn't work, but because the trade union wouldn't allow the bosses to use them on their members (or anything else come to that).

Satellites

No self-respecting spying nation should be without its own spy-in-the-sky satellites (SAMOS). The first ever was launched as you might have guessed, in California in 1961 and could, if it wanted, take either snaps of a whole continent, or of your mum and dad lying on the beach at Skegness – and develop the pics on board (without sending them to the chemist). It had a little chum satellite called a MIDAS which, through its infrared detection kit could tell if someone that it didn't like had launched a missile.

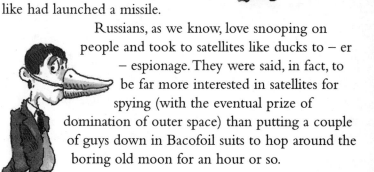

Russians, as we know, love snooping on people and took to satellites like ducks to – er – espionage. They were said, in fact, to be far more interested in satellites for spying (with the eventual prize of domination of outer space) than putting a couple of guys down in Bacofoil suits to hop around the boring old moon for an hour or so.

Nothing New Under the Sun

Spying from the sky is not new, however. In the nineteenth century, they sent hot air balloons to snoop on the enemy and during the Second World War, cameras were standard equipment on all fighter aircraft. Now everyone's up there, literally hundreds of satellites – Russian, Chinese, South African . . . crikey, I wouldn't mind betting the Irish have one – all frantically taking pictures of each other and where they came from. As for Britain, we're old hands at it. Despite the end of the Cold War, there's even a massive concrete bunker under sleepy Northwood Hills just north of London, where Navy boffins keep a constant watch on Soviet ships, submarines, planes or whatever (called OPCON).

Satellites linked to ships and massively sensitive ground stations are now responsible for 85% of all surveillance. Massive computers work day and night making sense of the jumble of signals they transmit. The British Government's Communication Centre at Cheltenham employs a staggering 140,000 people and costs us a cool 15 billion quid a year. Practically nothing escapes their notice (they could probably even spot you passing a note under the desk if they wanted.)

By the Way

These days, cameras 200 miles above the earth can focus on stuff no larger than a foot long. The US Big Bird satellites, probably the best in the world, can read a newspaper headline or tell if a person's wearing glasses.

Did you know that in Russia the FSB (son of KGB) are making all companies install a box (called STORM) so that everything they send through the internet can be monitored? Did you know that in the States there have been various attempts by the government to stop ordinary people using codes on the net? If they get their way they will soon only allow those to which they have a back door key, or those that are so weedy that almost anyone can decode them.

In other words – BIG BROTHER WILL SOON BE WATCHING US ALL!

Russia Plays Our Games

There is strong evidence to believe that throughout the 1980s up to 20,000 Russian agents snuck into the West with the most odd instructions. They were to buy or steal any kids' computer games they could find and take them back to Moscow to be examined by their boffins. The poor old Russkies had fallen so far behind with their computer technology, that even the simplest computer toys yielded programming information that was a complete revelation to them. For all we know over here, the same chip used to steer a toy dumper-truck could have been adapted to guide a lethal missile (scary or what!). The joke is, through examining all these toys and games they practically caught up with the West – and, much to the distress of the CIA, it cost them virtually nothing.

SPY TALK

If you're thinking of becoming a spy one day, you'd better get familiar with a few of the words they use else they'll find you out right away. Even if you don't, it might help when reading books about espionage or watching all those 007 movies.

Ag and Fish: This stands for the British Ministry of Agriculture and Fisheries. What's that got to do with spies? In World War I it was used as a cover address for intelligence staff. Throughout the fifties (the Cold War) many resting spies had desk jobs at the ministry and it was understood that when a spy was said to be at Ag and Fish it meant he had 'gone to ground'.

Agent Provocateur: An agent sent into another country to stir up trouble.

Biographic Leverage: Posh term for good old fashioned blackmail.

Black-Bag Jobs: No it's not your boyfriend or girlfriend, it's part of an agent's everyday work – everything from burglary to bribery to kidnapping to even murder.

Bleep Box: A method of telephone tapping, by which codes and frequencies enable the operative to break into various telephone networks. Used by most intelligence services.

Blown: The term used when an agent is found out. When an agent squeals on his own sub-agent – wife, mistress, parrot etc. he is said to have 'blown his own strumpet' which is about as close as a spy gets to a joke!

Bugging: Listening-in when you shouldn't.

Burnt: An agent who has been discovered and becomes – how shall I say? – surplus to requirements.

C: The head of the British Secret Service.

Cacklebladder: The term used for making a person look dead who isn't really (chicken blood etc.). This is often used for blackmailing and forcing a confession from enemy agents.

Cannon: The bloke whose job it is to steal back the money given to an enemy agent for information. Not a career for the faint-hearted.

The Centre: Nickname for the KGB headquarters, Moscow.

Cheka: Extraordinary Commission for the Struggle against Counter Revolution and Sabotage – the predecessor to the KGB.

Cobbler: The guy you go to for a forged passport.

CIA: American Central Intelligence Agency (nicknamed 'the Company').

Cousins: The British nickname for the CIA.

Defector: Someone who runs away from either their cause or their country (or wife).

Demote Maximally: To kill someone (isn't that completely brilliant?).

Dirty Tricks: Term used for the darker antics of the CIA.

Disinformation: Anything that is designed to discredit or fool your enemy. False documents, false messages, smear tactics – you name them.

Doctor: The Police. Hence, when arrested, 'he's gone to the doctor.'

Dubok: Hiding place for KGB agents' messages – could be anything from a milk bottle on a step to a rabbit-hole (on the steppes).

Espionage: The use of spies.

FBI: Federal Bureau of Intelligence – America's secret counter espionage service.

Field: The particular area in which a particular spy works.

The Firm: The British Secret Service (also a term for the Royal Family★).

★*Who probably aren't spies.*

Fix: CIA term meaning to blackmail or con rotten.

Fluttered: To be quizzed by a lie detector.

Footwarmer: An amplifier used in radio transmission.

Fumigating: Checking a building for bugs (electronic ones).

Fur-lined seat cover: Obscure reference to an agent who has a female passenger in tow. (Eh?)

In the Game: Someone in the intelligence industry.

On the Game: Ask your mates.

GCHQ: Government Communications Headquarters. Britain's listening-in centre at Cheltenham.

Going Private: Leaving the Secret Service (see dangerous things to do.)

Harmonica Bug: Weeny microphone that goes in a telephone.

Hospital: Prison – how appropriate!

Illegals: Top-notch Russian spies sent with false passports to foreign countries.

Komitet Gosudarstvennoy Bezopasnosti or KGB (thank God for abbreviations): The Soviet Committee for State Security.

Legend: A fake life-story used by a spy as cover.

Lion-tamer: The man used to 'calm down' a sacked agent who starts making threats. Not usually a very nice chap.

M: The head of the British secret service (but only in Bond movies).

Miss Moneypenny: His personal secretary.

Magpie Board: A small bunch of keys, wires, knives, small tools even a miniature transmitter, carried by agent to aid escape if captured.

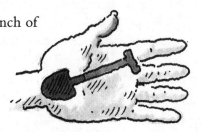

Measles: A murder that's done so well that it looks as if the poor chap (or lady) died of natural causes.

MI5: Britain's Counter-Intelligence Bureau.

MI6: Britain's Secret Service, London based but operating mainly abroad.

Mole: An agent sent to work with the enemy or rival company in order to spill their secrets.

Mozhno Girls: Pretty girls recruited by the KGB to seduce Western targets and report back to base on their pillow talk.

Music Box: Radio transmitter.

Musician: Its operator.

Naked: Term for operating alone without any help from outside.

Nash: From a Russian word meaning to belong to one's own side.

News: Usually bad news.

Orchestra: Long term agents who remain dormant until being asked, blackmailed or bullied into service.

Pavement Artists: Surveillance teams.

Peep: The bloke who takes secret photographs, especially in rotten conditions.

SMILE PLEASE

Piano Study: Radio operation.

Piscine: The nickname for the French Secret Service (because it's next to a swimming pool).

Plumbing: All the undercover work necessary to set up and stage a major operation.

Pudding: Sarcastic term used by Western agents for the United Nations.

In the Pudding Club: Inside UN headquarters.

Quick Trip Round the Horn: An agent's radio check on what's going on.

Radar Button: Gizmo which can pinpoint its carrier's position anywhere in the world. Usually used by his controller to get him out of trouble if absolutely necessary.

Raven: A handsome dude used to seduce women in the line of duty (rough job but someone's got to do it).

Safe House: Somewhere secret where an agent can seek sanctuary if things get a bit hot.

Sanction: Approval for a killing.

Scalp-Hunters: Experts whose job it is to tell genuine defectors from fakes. They will also advise on anyone who even looks like they are about to make a dash for it.

Setting-up: Trapping someone by secret agents. Typical scenario – employing a pretty girl to lure the prey into a hotel bedroom bristling with microphones and cameras. Favourite of the KGB.

Shoe: A false passport.

Sisters: Lower ranks of female spy.

Sleeper: An agent who works in deep cover for years in a foreign country (see Gordon Lonsdale).

Soap: Well-known truth drug.

Son et Lumière: The information on camera and microphone that you get from a set-up.

Spoofing: Snooping on secret establishments from the air. Term used after the World War II. Special high-flying planes with the latest in long-distance digital cameras are used.

Spook: Agent or intelligence gatherer.

Stable: The term for the list of 'ladies' available to do 'setting-up' operations. Often high-class prostitutes.

Sweetener: Money or gift used to persuade a 'target'.

Taxi: Gay version of the ladies in the 'stable'.

Thermal Detector: A gadget which can tell where someone has been lying or sitting (measuring bum heat presumably).

Thirty-Threes: Emergencies.

Turned Agent: Someone who changes sides.

Walk-in: Someone who offers his services or simply gives information without being asked.

What's your twenty?: Where the hell are you?

XX Committee: Double-cross committee set up to control double or turned agents in World War II.

Zoo: Police Station.

So there you go – all set up to be a spy. Now you must decide who to spy on (and who for).

...AND NOW

The whole intelligence business since the end of the Cold War (which America seems to have won hands down) should, if you think about it, be withering. The fifty years of fist-shaking between the superpowers is over – the clumsy commies are beat good and proper (except for China) – for the time being! Ninety per cent of all espionage in the last fifty years was all about the Americans trying to find out secret-type things about the Russians, and vice versa, while, of course, both were trying their level best to stop the other doing the same. It was all like a massive, hopelessly expensive, unnecessarily complex game of chess with neither side revealing its moves. It got so intense that the Yanks, for

instance, spent more time and money looking for 'reds under the bed' (whether they were there or not) than attending to their own problems at home. As for the Russians, we all know the terminal fix they got themselves into by not spending enough time glancing at what was going on in their own backyard.

You'd think that with whole countries like Poland, Hungary and East Germany at last throwing off the vice-like hug of the great Russian bear, the need for the massive Soviet intelligence agencies would be greatly reduced. This was true to a point but despite the massive cutbacks, after the Cold War, in military and intelligence staffing (resulting in a lot of spies in the dole queue) both Russia and America find it necessary to get their intelligence services back up to strength to make sure they aren't caught with their pants down ever again. It's a known fact that both sides are catching more spies now than they ever did during the Second World War. And there's always China.

But all that's understood. More important are all the threats that now seem almost more serious than anything the Russians or Yanks could do to each other. Terrorism, drug trafficking, international financial crime, industrial espionage are all alive and kicking and gaining strength wherever you look. And there's still China.

Whereas weapons always used to be difficult to get hold of, you or I, or even the Archbishop of blinking Canterbury, could go and buy just about anything from a pea shooter to a nuclear missile tomorrow through the Internet, providing we've enough in our piggy banks. We could even, if the money stretched far enough, have a private army fully tooled up and ready for a scrap in a matter of weeks – so watch it!

The cost of fighting the drug war in the States topped thirteen billion dollars in 1994 and massive markets are opening up everywhere you look – especially in all those ex-Communist countries which have had the door on the old fun cupboard nailed on so tight for so, so long. The amount of drugs coming into Britain, by the way, that are seized wouldn't keep the demand satisfied for a split second – that's how bad it is.

As for terrorism; the rise of religious fanaticism that seems to be spreading its tentacles throughout a world that really would prefer to do without it, is so scary I can hardly talk about it.

As for finding out what all these guys are up to; unlike the old days, it's all become more difficult. Terrorists don't just call each other up from their mum's phone any more and drug barons don't fax each other every five minutes, and no self-respecting arms dealers would go near a telex machine – oh no. They're all into the most sophisticated methods of communication (like pigeons), most times outwitting those who are trying to catch 'em.

Who's Listening?

As we speak, an enormous battle is going on in cyberspace between all the intelligence services that are trying to control the internet, and all the civil liberty organisations that don't want them to. Snooping on our ordinary telephone lines has been going on for ages in this country from major sites like Cornwall and the Yorkshire Dales. They link up with others around the world.

These days the way intelligence agencies work has been changing. All that tapping, bugging, mail rustling and office-breaking is old hat. The perfect spy now works with ridiculously high focused mikes, laser beams and untraceable mobile phones. Best (or worst) of all, use of this equipment often doesn't require a Home Office warrant.

But hang on, now all this is in danger of going out of date too. More and more communication goes via the net using e-mails and ISDNs (Integrated Service Digital Networks) and it is notoriously unsafe. The trouble is, just as all the security services use the very latest in computer equipment, all the same stuff is available to you and me too. Not only that, you can buy software to create some of the most sophisticated codes known to man – off the shelf. The cat is still stalking the mouse but, day by day the mouse is in danger of becoming bigger and cleverer than the cat.

Big Brother

Did you know that a ring of steel surrounds the City of London. Cameras record the registration plate of every car entering or leaving?

Did you know that throughout Britain there are so many cameras watching us that soon all our faces (including yours) will be entered onto a national database?

NO: 179/325/678·4

End Piece

Before you all go and hide under the bed, let me assure you that the future isn't all doom and gloom – far from it. Believe it or not, it has suddenly dawned on our brilliant world leaders that the enemy of mankind might not actually be each other . . . but international crime. Instead of wasting all their not-very-hard-earned cash on trying to second-guess what their counterparts are up to, the great powers are beginning to pool their resources. Who knows, you might even get a situation where the heads of MI6 and the KGB go out for a pint and a game of darts together. Having said that, I bet our spies would be able to find out who'd win (and make the necessary adjustments).

THE SHORT AND
BLOODY
HISTORY
OF

Stand and deliver

HIGHWAYMEN

John Farman

Have you ever wondered what highwaymen did during the day? And do you know who the most devious highwayman was, or which roads used to be the most dangerous in Britain? John Farman's ready to stand and deliver all the answers, so take a closer look at this short and bloody history of highwaymen!

£2.99   0 09 940711 6

THE SHORT AND
BLOODY
HISTORY
OF

All aboard, Landlubbers!

PIRATES

John Farman

Have you ever wondered why pirates wore gold earrings, or where the saying 'sick as a parrot' came from? And do you know who the cruellest pirate in history was?

John Farman's got all the answers, so come aboard for his short and bloody history of the day-to-day life of pirates!

£2.99   0 09 940709 4

THE SHORT AND
BLOODY
HISTORY
OF

Fancy a joust?

KNIGHTS

John Farman

Have you ever wondered how knights managed to walk, let alone fight, covered from head
to foot in metal? And have you heard about the
knights who became addicted to jousting?
Or the knight who was rescued by a monkey?
It's all in John Farman's short and bloody
history of knights. So arm yourself for a
fact attack!

£2.99   0 09 940712